BANANAS

Sam McBratney

Illustrated by
Alexa Rutherford

Series Editors
Steve Barlow and Steve Skidmore

Bananas

When this play begins, a grandfather is telling his granddaughter about something that happened over forty years ago, when he was a skinny boy called Geordy.

Trevor Moorhead is the fastest gun in the street. Geordy and Marcus would like to outdraw Moorhead and fill him full of holes, but their problem is that they haven't got a fancy cowboy gun in a holster like Moorhead has.

The two boys set about solving their problem. They decide that they could probably outdraw Moorhead by using bananas as guns – but food is still very expensive in the years after the Second World War, and Geordy and Marcus can't afford to buy them.

They steal the bananas. And that's when things become complicated for Geordy. He discovers in a mysterious way that you can run from the bad things you do in life, but you can't hide...

The Main Characters

Granddaughter
A lively girl of about ten. With her grandfather, she remains on stage throughout the play.

Grandfather
A man in his fifties. He is telling his granddaughter about something that happened when he was about her age.

Geordy
Geordy is grandfather when he was young. He manages to get into all sorts of trouble during the play, which worries him a lot.

Marcus
Marcus is Geordy's friend. They spend much of the play working out how to get the better of Trevor Moorhead.

Moorhead
Moorhead always gets his sums right and he always has the best toys. Geordy and Marcus are a bit jealous of him.

Sheila
Sheila is Geordy's younger sister. She'll tell on him if she gets half a chance.

Other characters with smaller parts are **Geordy's mother** and **father**, and a **fruit and vegetable seller**.

Grandfather

Granddaughter

Geordy

Marcus

Moorhead

Sheila

Scene 1

(Grandfather and Granddaughter are on stage. Granddaughter is brandishing a space gun. She stalks and shoots Grandfather.)

Granddaughter: Kapow!

Grandfather: Oooh-aaaaggggh! *(He pretends to be shot.)*

Granddaughter: You don't go "ooh-aagh", Grandad, you're disintegrated.

Grandfather: *(Picking himself up)* Oh, sorry. That thing disintegrates people, does it?

Granddaughter: It's a power-blaster. It's for shooting aliens from outer space.

Grandfather:	What happens if the aliens are friendly?
Granddaughter:	Grandad – I don't shoot them if they're friendly, do I? They only get shot if they're going to take over the Earth. Didn't you have one of these when you were my age?
Grandfather:	Did I have a space-age power-blaster? Are you kidding?
Granddaughter:	Did Grandma?
Grandfather:	I didn't know your Grandma then. I shouldn't think so – girls didn't have guns. They had dolls.
Granddaughter:	Yeuch!
Grandfather:	There was a boy down our street had a six-gun, though. Trevor Moorhead. Do you know what a six-gun is?
Granddaughter:	Yeah – Cowboys and Indians and all that. The Lone Ranger had one.
Grandfather:	The Lone Ranger had two – one on each hip. *(He borrows the space gun and pretends to draw with it.)* The whole idea was to be quick on the draw.
Granddaughter:	Was Trevor Moorhead quick on the draw?
Grandfather:	He sure was. And he used to give the gun a kind of fancy twirl before sticking it back in the holster.
Granddaughter:	*(Twirling the gun)* Like this?
Grandfather:	*(Taken aback)* Er, yes. My friend Marcus and I were mad with jealousy every time we saw him …

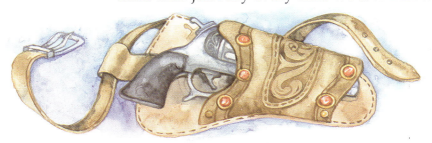

Scene 2

(A street. A boy enters, blowing imaginary smoke from his revolver. Marcus and Geordy follow him, watching with envy. Grandfather and Granddaughter watch from the side of the stage.)

Granddaughter: Is that Moorhead?

Grandfather: That's him. Big show off. And *that (he indicates Geordy)* is me.

Granddaughter: You were a bit skinny then, weren't you, Grandad?

Grandfather: Ssssh. Watch.

Moorhead: Do you see the smoke? That's the gunpowder does that.

Geordy: It's caps, Moorhead, only caps.

Marcus: You'd think the gun was real to hear you talk, Moorhead.

Moorhead: Would you and Marcus dare to draw against me?

Geordy: I'll draw against you.

Marcus: So will I.

Moorhead: Come on, then.

Geordy: Right. You wait here and I'll get a gun.

(Marcus watches Geordy go off. Moorhead practises twirling his gun. Marcus looks over to where Geordy left the stage.)

Moorhead: What's he up to, then?

Marcus: He's digging in his dad's vegetable patch. Can't see what he's got. He's put it in his pocket.

Moorhead: *(In a cowboy drawl)* Kinda pitiful, ain't it?

(Geordy re-enters with a carrot sticking out of his pocket.)

Geordy: Okay, when Marcus hits the fence with a stick, we draw. I'm gonna fillya fulla holes.

Moorhead: *(Smiling)* I'm ready when you are.

(They face one another, crouched, ready to draw and very tense. Marcus hits the fence and the carrot flies out of Geordy's hand as he draws.)

Moorhead: Got ya! You're too slow.

Geordy: You've been practising, that's why.

Marcus: And you had a real gun.

Moorhead: *(Smirking)* Oh yes, blame it on the carrots. You're too slow, you're too slow.

(Moorhead swaggers away, clearly thinking that he's the fastest draw on Planet Earth.)

Geordy: I'd like to plug him so full of holes you could read the paper through him.

Marcus: He's too quick. There's no way you'll do it with one of your dad's carrots.

Geordy: Right, that settles it! I'm going to ask my dad for a six-gun when he comes in tonight …

(Geordy and Marcus leave the stage while Grandfather and Granddaughter talk.)

Grandfather: Marcus and I were bitterly disappointed that we hadn't managed to fill Moorhead full of daylight. He was in the same class as us two and always seemed to get top marks in all the tests. He wrote his homework in red ink from a fountain pen with a real gold nib. What can you do with a kid like that?

(Granddaughter mimes "disintegrating" Moorhead with her blaster.)

Grandfather: Exactly. I *had* to get a six-gun, so I tackled my dad.

Scene 3

(*That evening at tea. Geordy, his sister Sheila and their parents are sitting round the table. Grandfather and Granddaughter are still watching from the side of the stage.*)

Geordy: Dad, would you buy me a six-gun in a holster?

Father: A what in a what?

Geordy: A six-gun in a holster. I could share it with Sheila and we wouldn't fight over it.

Sheila: I don't want a stupid old gun.

Father: So who do you want to shoot?

Geordy:	Ah, come on, Dad!
Mother:	Do you think you father's *made* of money? You got new pyjamas last week.
Geordy:	(*In disgust*) Pyjamas, pyjamas! What use are pyjamas?
Mother:	You'll think more of pyjamas when the winter comes, my lad.
Geordy:	Ah go on, Dad, Trevor Moorhead has one in a holster and you can even tie it down to your leg.
Father:	And when Trevor Moorhead gets the measles I suppose you'll want me to buy you them, too.
Geordy:	I never get anything!
Mother:	(*Quietly, firmly*) You got pyjamas.
Granddaughter:	Why didn't you want pyjamas, Grandad?
Grandfather:	Because I couldn't shoot Moorhead with a pair of pyjamas, could I – I wanted a six-gun in a holster. Anyway, when the rest of the family left the kitchen, I stayed behind feeling as grumpy as could be. I got a stool for myself, and climbed up to the cupboard. And I took a handful of biscuits out of a packet and slipped them into my pocket. Then I went outside.
Granddaughter:	You mean … you *stole* them?
Grandfather:	Well – yes. But it was to pay them back for buying me pyjamas instead of a six-gun. And then – next day – something happened. Marcus came out to play with a banana sticking out of his right pocket …

Marcus: Watch this. Are you watching?

Geordy: Go on, let's see you.

> *(Marcus makes one smooth, lovely motion and Geordy is staring down the barrel of a banana.)*

Marcus: What do you think?

Geordy: Beautiful!

Marcus: It's the shape, you see. A carrot hasn't got a curve in it.

Geordy: Give me a go.

(The banana changes hands. Geordy draws.)

Marcus: What a draw! That was even quicker than mine!

Geordy: *(Loudly, waving the banana)* Bang! Where are you, Moorhead? Come out, come out!

Marcus: *(Shouting)* You're dead meat, Moorhead!

Geordy: Ah no, look what's happened. The banana's gone all squelchy. Have you any more?

Marcus: No. My mum got five off the priest, but we ate them.

Geordy: Well, we can't draw against Moorhead with this thing. Has the priest got any more?

Marcus: He's got everything – cabbages, pineapples, pears and all. Some lorry lost its load and he brought the whole lot cheap to sell in the church hall. He's selling them now.

Geordy: Maybe he would give us a free one. Would he?

Marcus: I'll ask him. Come on …

Granddaughter: Grandad – are you telling me you couldn't get a *banana*?

Grandfather: This wasn't long after the war, you know. It wasn't easy to get a banana in those days. People didn't have the money to buy them. Anyway, Marcus and I raced as hard as we could to the church hall. Near the gates I began to slow down.

Marcus: What's wrong? What's keeping you?

Geordy: Nothing, you go on.

Marcus: You're afraid.

Geordy: I'm not afraid, but they wouldn't give me one because I'm a Protestant. You go in yourself.

Marcus: Don't be daft. Wait there, then.

(Marcus goes offstage, into the hall. A lady comes onstage with boxes of fruit on a small handbarrow. The lady parks the barrow and waves to Geordy, who waves back. Marcus returns.)

Marcus: No use, they're all gone. He's only got turnips and green things left.

Geordy: Turnips is no use. *(He points.)* Do you see that barrow over there? She's got bananas. Got any money?

Marcus: No, I have not, where would I get money? I'll go and keep the woman talking and you swipe them. Or do you want to do the talking and I'll swipe them?

Geordy: You mean … pinch her bunch of bananas?

Marcus: It's the only way if we're going to plug Moorhead.

13

Geordy: Could we not just pinch *one?*

Marcus: We need one each. And an extra one in case they go squelchy on us.

Geordy: *(After a pause)* All right then. I'll do the talking and you swipe them. Just don't let her see you doing it – okay?

(During the following speeches, Marcus and Geordy argue – silently – about who will do what. Eventually Marcus hides and Geordy slowly and nervously approaches the lady who's standing by the stall.)

Granddaughter: Grandad, it's wrong to pinch bananas. I'm surprised at you.

Grandfather: Oh I know, I know. I *knew* it was wrong to pinch bananas. I couldn't help thinking of Miss Hetherington.

Granddaughter: Who was *she?*

Grandfather: She was my lovely Sunday School teacher, and she must have been all of sixteen years old.

Granddaughter: Did you like Miss Hetherington?

Grandfather: I was dyin' about her! Sunday was the only day when I combed my own hair. She used to use so much perfume that you could taste it as well as smell it. I knew in my heart that Miss Hetherington would be sad if I stole bananas. But … I thought of Moorhead and that decided me.

Scene 6

(Geordy is standing by the lady with the barrow; Marcus is crouched down, hiding, but visible to the audience. While Geordy and the lady are talking, Marcus slides in behind her back and stuffs a bunch of bananas under his jumper. Then he scuttles off.)

Geordy: *(Nervously)* Missus, have you got some old cabbage leaves you don't want for my rabbit?

Lady: Cabbage? I didn't know they ate cabbage.

Geordy: Well … it's a bit sick.

Lady: Off its grub, eh? Is it a he or a she?

Geordy: I don't know.

Lady: What do you call it?

Geordy: Er … Sheila!

Lady: Must be a she, then, mustn't it? I don't know many fellas called Sheila. I used to have a big buck rabbit once and I was scared to go near him. Here. *(She tosses a cabbage to Geordy.)* Take that.

Geordy: But that's a whole cabbage. I haven't got any money.

Lady: Don't worry, it's for a good cause. By the time Sheila gets through that lot she'll be as right as rain.

Geordy: *(Backing away)* Thanks. Thanks very much.

Lady: You're welcome, son. *(She goes off, pushing the barrow.)*

Scene 7

(Geordy is on stage, holding his cabbage. Marcus comes on with the bulge of a bunch of bananas under his jumper.)

Geordy: Did you get them?

Marcus: Certainly I got them. I got the whole bunch!

Geordy: She gave me a cabbage. That woman gave me a whole cabbage for my sick rabbit.

Marcus: So what are you worried about?

Geordy: My rabbit's not sick. I haven't even got a rabbit! What am I going to do with this?

Marcus: Stick it in that litter bin.

Geordy: You're not supposed to waste good food. Miss Hetherington says you should send it away to poor people in far countries.

(Marcus takes the cabbage and dumps it in the litter bin.)

Geordy: *(Pointing to the bananas)* What are we going to do with them? We can't walk into the house with a bunch of bananas.

Marcus: I see what you mean. Somebody'll eat them.

Geordy: That's *not* what I mean – they'll want to know where we got them. Bananas don't grow on trees, you know, not round here they don't.

Marcus: Quit panicking, we'll hide them.

Geordy: We could bury them.

Marcus: No, slugs might eat them. You know that big hedge in front of your house? We'll push them into the middle of that until after tea.

Geordy: Okay.

Marcus: And I'll be round after tea as soon as I can. *(Shooting with banana, and shouting)* You're doomed, Moorhead. You're doomed!

(Geordy and Marcus go off.)

Granddaughter: Grandad, that was mean.

Grandfather: I know – I felt guilty at once. But it was too late by then. There was worse to come when I got in …

Scene 8

(Geordy's mother and sister Sheila are waiting for him at home. He rushes in.)

Geordy: Mam, I'm home.

Mother: *(Grimly)* Good. I'm glad you're home because there's something I want you to see. It's a packet of biscuits. Or maybe I should say it *was* a packet of biscuits.

Sheila: Greedy gorb.

Geordy: *(Trying to make excuses)* Mam, I didn't want pyjamas!

Mother: You stole those biscuits!

Sheila: Eight biscuits, I counted the missing ones.

Geordy: Yes, but …

Mother: But nothing! Those biscuits were for all of us, the whole family, and how anybody could be so rotten and selfish is beyond me. Where are they?

Geordy: I don't know.

Sheila: That means he ate them.

Geordy: But I could have taken the whole packet and you wouldn't have noticed.

Mother: Would I not, you cheeky article! Am I to say you're a good boy because you only stole ten biscuits instead of twenty? It's a clip on the ear you need, my lad. There'll not be *one* of those biscuits for you, not so much as a crumb. And what is Miss Hetherington going to say when I tell her about this?

Geordy: You'd better not tell her. You'd better not!

Mother: Well, have you learned your lesson about stealing things?

Geordy: *(Calm now)* Yes I have.

Mother: If you've learned your lesson, then … Say you're sorry and you'll not do it again.

Geordy: I'm sorry and I'll not do it again.

Granddaughter: Were you really sorry?

Grandfather: Well, sort of – but I still had to prove I was faster than Moorhead, didn't I?

Granddaughter: Why?

Grandfather: Well, it was a point of honour.

Granddaughter: Oh, that.

Grandfather: Anyway, we met up after tea.

Scene 9

(Geordy, Marcus and Moorhead in the street. Moorhead and Marcus are facing each other, ready to draw; Geordy is standing by the fence nearby.)

Moorhead: Same rules as before?

Marcus: Same rules as before. When Geordy hits the fence, we draw.

Moorhead: Your hand's too close to your gun.

Marcus: I'm not touching the handle, Moorhead. You're allowed your hand as close as you like so long as you don't touch it, okay?

Moorhead: I'm ready when you are.

Geordy: *(Hitting fence)* Go!

Marcus: I beat you!

Moorhead: You never did! You've got no caps, mine just sounded slow.

Geordy: I'll take you on, Moorhead.

(Geordy walks forward. He has a banana in each pocket.)

Moorhead: You've got two guns.

Geordy: *(Tossing away a banana)* Right, that's us even. Ready when you are.

(They face each other. Marcus hits the fence and they draw.)

21

Geordy:	I got you!
Moorhead:	You didn't, you didn't, I shot you in the head.
Geordy:	Moorhead, you were full of daylight before you even got your gun out.
Moorhead:	You're refusin' to die, you're refusin' to die!
Marcus:	That's because we got you first and you can't take it.
	(Moorhead walks away in a huff.)
Marcus:	*(Calling after him)* You're not getting any of our bananas, Moorhead.
Moorhead:	I don't want them, we've got plenty in our house. And we've got figs! And you're two cheaters because a banana's got no trigger.
	(When Moorhead has gone, Geordy's mum calls from offstage.)
Mother:	Geordy!
Marcus:	There's your mum. You want to take a banana with you?
Geordy:	No! *(More calmly)* You eat them.
Marcus:	See you in the morning.
	(Marcus and Geordy go off.)
Granddaughter:	Honestly, Grandad! You stole the biscuits from your mam and the bananas from that lady, just so you could show off.
Grandfather:	Ah, but you've not heard the rest of the story yet. Look what happened that evening.

Scene 10

(Geordy goes into his house. There is a parcel on the table. His mother and father are smiling. Sheila is also present.)

Geordy: What's in the parcel?

Father: Oh, some wee thing I picked up down the town.

Sheila: I know what it is, don't I, Mam?

Geordy: Who is it for?

Father: If you're that nosy you may open it and see.

(Geordy opens the parcel, which contains a gun, holster, belt, and even caps. He is overwhelmed.)

Geordy: You got me one. *(He pauses.)* Can I put it on?

Father: That's the general idea.

(Geordy puts it on.)

Sheila: It's half mine, isn't it, Dad? He's got to share it with me.

Mother: What do you want with a silly old cowboy gun? *(To Geordy)* And where do you think you're off to?

Geordy: To see Marcus.

Mother: Get away up to your bed – which is where Marcus is already, I'm sure. And don't you go shooting those caps until the morning comes …

Grandfather: Well, when I went to bed that night, I laid the six-gun on a pillow by my head so I could feel it all over if I happened to wake up in the dark. And what a gun it was – silver barrel, pearly handle, leather holster, fancy buckle and fancy belt – the full works. There was even a sheriff's tin star to go with it. Do you know what a sheriff was?

Granddaughter: *(Patiently)* Yes, Grandad – I know what a sheriff was. What happened about the bananas?

Grandfather: I'm coming to the bananas. That night, the night I got the gun, I was as rich as I ever wanted to be. But before I fell asleep, my mind got to asking some questions. What had I *done* to deserve this great bolt of joy all of a sudden? And the answer was simple: I'd stolen one of my dad's carrots, told a double lie about a sick rabbit, eaten half a packet of family biscuits, and pinched five bananas as well as wasting a good cabbage. Even I could see there was something wrong here. All the Methodists I knew, including Mum, Dad and Miss Hetherington, spoke with one voice about such matters: you could run from the bad things you did in life, but you could not hide. So why had I been rewarded with a brand-new six-gun? The answer was terribly clear to me. There'd been some sort of mistake up in heaven.

Granddaughter: Well at least you were feeling guilty again. Serves you right. What did you do?

Grandfather: What did I do! What would you do? I decided to say nothing …

Marcus: You want to go down and call for Moorhead?

Geordy: *(Without enthusiasm)* Nah.

Marcus: What do you want to do, then?

Geordy: I dunno.

Marcus: It's the bananas, that's what's wrong with you.

Geordy: It's not the bananas!

Marcus: 'Tis. Well, they're eaten now, so they belong to history.

Geordy: I know they're history. I know that!

(Pause. Marcus twirls Geordy's gun.)

Marcus: Look, it's all right about the bananas, I told Father Avery about them. He said it was bad, true enough, but there's worse things.

Geordy: You what? You told *who*?

Marcus: Father Avery. The priest.

Geordy: *(Thoroughly alarmed)* You've told the priest? You've gone and told the priest?

Marcus: It's all right, he knows about these things. People tell him about murders they've done and things like that.

Geordy: He'll tell on us, he'll tell on us!

Marcus: He'll not tell. It's confession, he doesn't tell anybody your business. *(He pauses.)* Except maybe God.

Geordy: God's not the problem! What about the greengrocer? And Miss Hetherington! You stupid eejit, you've gone and told the priest and he'll put everybody wise. *(More calmly)* I'm dead. He'll be down to see my dad. Half a packet of biscuits and now five bananas, I'll get skinned alive. And they'll give the gun to Sheila. I knew it was all too good to be true …

Granddaughter: Well? Did the priest come? What did your dad say?

Grandfather: No, the priest never came near us. He had more to worry about than a bunch of bananas, I'd say.

Granddaughter: You mean you got away with it? I knew it!

Grandfather: Well … Something happened. Something mysterious …

Scene 12

(In the house. A summer evening. Mother is working. She hears from outside three loud blasts of a van's horn. She sighs. Sheila and Geordy burst in.)

Sheila: Mam, Mam, it's the ice-cream van!

Geordy: *(Urgently)* Mam, can I have money for ice-cream?

Mother: You got one the day before yesterday.

Sheila: Everybody else is getting one.

Geordy: Come on, Mam!

Sheila: He's going to be away.

Mother: *(Handing over the money)* If you ask me, that ice-cream man should be shot.

(Sheila and Geordy speed off. Mother calls after them.)

Mother: Can I hear a "thank you", if you don't mind?

Sheila: *(From offstage)* Thanks, Mam. You wait for *me*, Geordy …

Granddaughter: Are you telling me you got an ice-cream as well?

Grandfather: Wait! *(He indicates the scene that is gathering.)*

Geordy: Who's got my six-gun? Where is it, Marcus?

Marcus: You've got it yourself. I gave it back to you when we all went home for ice-cream money.

Geordy: You did not.

Marcus: I did so! When we heard the van, I gave it you back.

Geordy: *(Standing)* Somebody's got my gun. Did you take it, Moorhead?

Marcus: I've got my own gun.

Geordy: Who's got my gun?

(The children exchange glances, and Geordy glares at Sheila.)

Sheila: I haven't got it either and you can search me, okay?

Geordy: *(Becoming distraught)* I left it on the pavement. Down there! Somebody must have it! *(The others drift away as he runs among them.)* One of you pinched my gun, so you did. One of you has it. You'd better give it back to me or I'm going to tell the police and they'll come and arrest you.

(Geordy's shouts and screeches bring out his mother.)

Mother: What are you doing, kicking up that racket in the street? Anybody would think it was the end of you!

Geordy: I've lost my gun!

Mother: Well it must be *somewhere*.

Geordy: It's not. *(In a bad temper)* I've *looked*.

Mother: Come inside! If you would look after your things properly you wouldn't get yourself into this state. Go on.

Geordy: Will Dad buy me another one?

Mother: No he will not indeed buy you another one. And if you ask me, he's not going to be too pleased to hear that you've gone and lost the one he did buy you. How are you going to explain that, I'd like to know?

Granddaughter: Did you ever find the gun?

Grandfather: No. Well, I suppose I did in a way, but it was too late.

Granddaughter: Where was it?

Grandfather: Can't you guess? It wasn't far away.

Granddaughter: No, I can't think where it was. In the house, maybe?

Grandfather: Well, the winter went by. In the turn of the year, my father – that's your great-grandfather – took the shears to the privet hedge in the front garden and gave it a good trim. And he came across the six-gun.

Granddaughter: It was in the hedge all the time!

Grandfather: It was still in its holster, although the fancy leather had now turned to a horrible green slime. The gun itself had rusted right through. A banana – or even a carrot – had more style than that awful-looking rusty old dud.

(While Grandfather is talking, Geordy comes on holding the rusty, dirty gun. He is followed by Moorhead and Marcus. He shows the gun to them. Marcus shrugs. Moorhead laughs. Father and Mother come in and put their hands on Geordy's shoulders. Sheila comes in.)

Grandfather: Of course, it was all clear to me now. On the night when the ice-cream man came I'd shoved the six-gun into the very hedge where Marcus and I had hidden the stolen bananas, and it had perished there. Something up in the sky had sorted out that earlier mistake. And justice had come down on me as quiet as the morning dew.

(Granddaughter reaches out for Grandfather's hand. At the same moment, Sheila takes Geordy's hand.)

THE END.

Teachers' Notes

Choosing Parts

Grandfather, Granddaughter, Geordy and Marcus should be played by confident readers. Moorhead, Sheila, Mother, Father and the Street-seller are slightly less demanding parts.

Putting On the Play

Of course, the play can simply be read around the class, or read using only a few props and actions. If you wish to put on a fully-staged production, the following notes may be helpful. Obviously, the use you make of these suggestions will vary depending on the time and resources available to your school.

For permission to put on a profit-making performance of *Bananas*, please contact the Editorial Department, Ginn & Co. Ltd, Prebendal House, Parson's Fee, Aylesbury, Bucks HP20 2QY.
(There is no need to apply for permission if you are not charging an entrance fee, but please let us know if you are putting on any performance of this play, as we would be interested to hear about it.)

Staging

The play can probably most readily be produced on a stage divided into three parts.
Upstage right or left could be set aside for Grandfather and Granddaughter (slightly raised if staging is available, with perhaps a sofa or chairs). The other upstage corner can then be used for the interior scenes with Geordy's family, who will need a dining table and chairs.

The downstage area should mostly be used for outdoor scenes such as the shoot-out, as this will bring most of the crucial scenes close to the audience; but there is no reason why 'upstage' scenes should not spill over into the downstage space.

Costumes

Grandfather and **Granddaughter** should be dressed in contemporary clothes. All the other characters should be dressed in the style of the late 1940s.
Geordy and **Marcus** should wear shorts, pullovers and long socks (the latter probably round their ankles). They will need sensible shoes, and their clothes should look well-used but not ragged.
Moorhead should be dressed like **Geordy** and **Marcus**, but more neatly.
Sheila would wear a print dress or a skirt and blouse, with ankle socks and sensible shoes.
Mother might have an apron, and **Father** could wear overalls.
The **Street-seller** should be well wrapped up in coat and scarf, and perhaps fingerless gloves.

Props

Flashy modern space-gun for **Granddaughter**.
Cowboy gun and holster for **Moorhead**.
A dirty big carrot for **Geordy**.
A stick for **Geordy and Marcus** to hit the fence with.
A bunch of bananas for various uses throughout the play.
A big cabbage for the **Street-seller** to give to Geordy.
A wheelbarrow or similar with fruit and vegetables for the **Street-seller**.
A box containing a gun and holster for **Geordy**.

Money for **Mother** to give to Geordy and Sheila for ice-cream.
A dirty, broken gun brought on at the end by **Geordy**.

Sound Effects

There is only one sound effect: three loud blasts of a horn, on tape, for the ice-cream van.

Follow-up Work

Research

Encourage the whole group to do some research into the period. Library books, papers and magazines of the period and videos of contemporary films should be useful resources. Subjects for research could includecostume and post-war austerity. It is important that children know about austerity so they understand why bananas are so hard to come by, and why Geordy feels so guilty about stealing them.
The play is set in Northern Ireland, but post-war austerity affected everyone, and the themes are universal. The religious divide is mentioned only once, and there is no awkwardness between the Catholic Marcus and the Protestant Geordy, but this question might be addressed if desired.

Group Discussion

Bananas focuses on wrongdoing, guilt and retribution. The group might go on to discuss such issues as:
• the worst thing I have ever done;
• the most embarrassing thing that has ever happened to me;
• a time when I wanted something as badly as Geordy wanted the six-gun.

Drama
Improvisation

This exercise is best done after discussing the issues as suggested above. In small groups, the children can agree to improvise a situation experienced by one of them. The child concerned can play himself or herself, and the others can take on other roles as appropriate. Each group can then perform its improvisation for the whole class.
Each of the group improvisations can be extended as suggested below.

Hot-seating

Each character in the improvisation in turn should sit and face the others. The others may ask the character questions to be answered in role. The object is to explore each character's perceptions of the situation.

Judgement Chair

Once hot-seating has been carried out and the results discussed, the characters can be invited to sit in the chair again. This time, each member of the group takesturns to pronounce judgement on the character in the chair.

Thought Alley

The group should go through the improvisation again to a crucial point, and then stop. The actors should then form a double line, and take it in turns to walk very slowly between the two lines. As each character passes, the others should take turns to say what he or she thinks this character would have been thinking at the moment the improvisation was halted. This can be repeated for as many characters as you wish.